Travels Across the Curriculum

Models for Interdisciplinary Learning

STEPHEN TCHUDI

SCHOLASTIC

Scholastic Canada Ltd.
123 Newkirk Road, Richmond Hill, Ontario, Canada L4C 3G5

Scholastic Inc.
730 Broadway, New York, NY 10003, USA

Ashton Scholastic Limited
Private Bag 1, Penrose, Auckland, New Zealand

Ashton Scholastic Pty Limited
PO Box 579, Gosford, NSW 2250, Australia

Scholastic Publications Ltd.
Villiers House, Clarendon Avenue, Leamington Spa,
Warwickshire CV32 5PR, UK

Cover photo © Peter Beck/MASTERFILE

6 5 4 3 2   Printed in USA   1 2 3 4/9

Canadian Cataloguing in Publication Data

Tchudi, Stephen
 Travels across the curriculum

ISBN 0-590-73810-0

1. Middle schools. 2. Education, Secondary
I. Title.

LB1051.D83 1991   370.15   C90-095724-7

Contents

Preface

Mostly because of some vague plans for a career in medicine, I majored in chemistry in college. About midway through my junior year I found myself decreasingly motivated in chemistry labs and increasingly interested in humanities. Sometime during my senior year I took a deep breath, dropped chemistry and pre-med, and switched to a track that led me to become a high school English teacher. For graduation someone gave me a copy of the *Oxford Anthology of English Literature* bearing the inscription: *To a successful union of the arts and sciences.*

Twenty-five years later that union still seems desirable. This book enables me to give voice to a simple proposition: that instead of fragmenting learning along disciplinary lines, as education has done for years, we need a *union* of disciplines through holistic, integrated, interdisciplinary learning.

I wouldn't limit this proposition to self-contained elementary school classrooms either; the specialized content areas of secondary schools should also be included. In fact, I see a need for more than a blending of disciplinary content. This book also shows ways of connecting students' personal growth and development with their burgeoning (inter)disciplinary knowledge.

Before I begin, I would like to add a note of explanation (and perhaps apology) to teachers in Canada, where this book is being published. I'm no stranger to Canada. I've taught (briefly) at the University of British Columbia, visited schools in several provinces, and worked with a number of Canadian teachers on publishing and classroom projects. I have, therefore, some knowledge of Canadian issues and concerns.

Yet most of the references in this text will be to U.S. schools. It's my belief that teachers in Canada are dealing with basically the same traditions and problems in learning as teachers in the United States are — and, for that matter, as those in England, New Zealand, and Australia. However, I don't want readers to suppose that I think conditions in the United States are identical to those elsewhere, or that ideas I see working there can be or should be exported. The examples and illustrations I use can only represent the range and limitations of my own experiences. I hope they won't be perceived as stereotypical U.S. culturocentrism.

Stephen Tchudi

Nobody knows anything anymore, eh?

I'm something of a newspaper addict. I read my morning paper with a coffee cup in one hand and scissors in the other. In my eclectic clipping files are many stories focusing on the current state of education.

Here was the headline in my paper the very day I began work on this manuscript:

SCHOOLS GET KNUCKLES RAPPED
Student Scores Decline

The story was familiar. Based on a report that U.S. college entrance examination results are continuing the steady decline of the past several decades, the newspaper blasted teachers for "failing to make the grade" with their students.

The same issue also contained a related story:

EXPERTS: Math Anxiety Reinforced by Education, Images

It reported that beginning in junior high, mathematics turns from "fun to foggy," leaving U.S. students "dead last" in an international assessment of mathematics skills. (Articles from the *Lansing State Journal*, 5/1/90, 1A, 3A.)

I know that in recent years school systems in Canada, Australia, Great Britain, and New Zealand have come in for similar attacks. In every subject area, in every discipline, students seem to fall short, know less than they did formerly, and be less knowledgeable than we want them to be.

"Geographically illiterate" youngsters have prompted Julie Hinds of Gannett News Service to query:

Where In the World Are Our Heads?

She found that students "fell flat on their atlases" in tests of geography. They didn't seem to know much more than how to locate the nearest shopping mall or video arcade. One of Hinds's interviewees blamed the problem on the decline of geography teaching in the schools, including "methodology that bores students out of their skulls" (*Lansing State Journal*, 9/26/88, 10).

Similar comments have also been made in other areas. Paul Gray, in an article in the *Chronicle of Higher Education* (5/18/88, B1) suggested that in math/science education:

Ignorance of Science and Technology
Poses a Threat to the Democratic Process Itself.

He argued that "our educational system has produced generation after generation of young people who are ignorant in science and incompetent in mathematics" and who are, therefore, unable to make intelligent voting decisions when faced with issues centering on science and technology.

The report of the prestigious Bradley Commission on History in Schools led to headlines declaring:

History Instruction Is 'In Crisis'

"We should stop pretending we are educating citizens when we really are not," said one of the report's authors, Professor Paul Gagnon of Harvard University (*Education Week,* 10/6/88, 7). He, too, thinks that school graduates lack the necessary perspective to vote intelligently. And other headlines highlight the same crisis (*Detroit Free Press,* 4/2/90, 1A):

History? It's Greek to Many Students

The English language arts fare no better. At one end of the literacy spectrum, people are worried about failures in basic skill instruction:

Illiteracy Takes a Toll on Business

Patricia Weir reminds us of the problem of adult illiteracy: "Imagine not being able to read this column, understand the comics, fill out a job application, or even look up a telephone number." She cites the effects on business of employees who make expensive errors due to illiteracy, or who can't even get the job done in the first place (*Detroit Free Press,* 2/12/88, 9A).

At the other end of the spectrum, English language arts teachers are faulted for their failure to instill knowledge of and love for classic authors like Dante, Chaucer, Dostoevsky, and Austen:

Today's Schools Ignore Literature

It seems that students generally draw a blank when asked to identify basic authors and literary works that are a part of our literary heritage (*Lansing State Journal,* 8/31/87, 3A). (It also turns out that the National Endowment for the Humanities spent $370,000 to discover this knowledge gap.)

It's common popular belief that today's youngsters can't read, write, think critically, do math, think scientifically, remember history, or fill in simple application blanks. A few writers, like Lewis Grizzard, blame the young people themselves, specifically their "orange hair," their listening to "loud music," and their preoccupation with music videos, sex, and drugs (*King Features Syndicate,* 10/15/90). Other writers blame phenomena as diverse as the dissolution of the family, the nuclear nightmare, poor adult role models, greed, and junk food. Whatever the causes, it seems to be widely believed that nobody knows anything anymore.

So what became of learning?

Stephen Jones, a writer for the *Detroit Free Press* who seems to be one of the few to think about these matters beyond headlines, quotes his father: "The older a man gets, the better he could swim as a boy" (10/26/89, 13A). He concludes that adults tend to glorify what they were able to do as youngsters, to inflate what they knew when they were young, and to exaggerate just how hard they hit the books.

Jones confesses:

> There aren't many things I remember actually learning in college . . . I remember going to class (most of the time) and reading a lot of books and listening to a lot of lectures. And I have great affection for the substantial education I absorbed outside class . . . But there is hardly anything concrete — facts, dates, formulas — that I recall learning in the classroom, hardly anything I can point to and say with certainty, I learned *that* in college.

He questions the traditional assumption that schools are the "dominant centers of learning in our lives" and reports he learned a lot from — horror of horrors! — films, television, and comic books.

Stephen Jones isn't proposing that we abandon schools and go to the movies, or educate ourselves through the funnies. He simply wants us to think cautiously about the alleged decline in learning.

So, apparently, does Greg Evans, the cartoonist who draws *Luann* (see page 10). What's the point of learning all this stuff in school, his teenage character asks, if none of it will be remembered afterward?

My son, the ten year old, came home from school recently with a joke on the same topic: "Did you hear about the five minute university?"

I hadn't.

"Well, they say that a few years after you graduate from college, you can only remember five minutes worth of knowledge. This new place is just going to teach the five minutes worth."

He paused. "And if you stay for two more minutes, they'll give you a law degree."

I don't want to argue whether learning is or is not in decline, whether kids nowadays are smarter or dumber than their parents, whether they know more or less math, geography, English, science, or history than they used to. But I find the headlines unpersuasive and unscientific. There's a great deal of reminiscing about "good old days" which, I suspect, never existed. And schools are frequently judged on the basis of standardized examinations which focus narrowly on the type of factual textbook knowledge that most people are going to forget anyway.

Furthermore, these days there's a curiously narrow-minded equation of education and making money. Much of the talk of training for "good citizenship" translates into schooling that will get people jobs and help restore the trade balance between the West and Japan. While I'm all in favor of jobs and a healthy trade balance, it seems quite unfair and even damaging to leap to the conclusion that problems with the economy can somehow be traced directly to whether or not students recognize the names of Dostoevsky, Sri Lanka, Pythagoras, or Boyle.

What seems to me especially disturbing about the headlines and nostalgia I've mentioned is that the writers look at education, as Marshall McLuhen would say, "through a rearview mirror." Many of their proposals for reform aren't new and visionary at all; they simply call for a redoubling of efforts that never succeeded in the first place.

There is much talk of increased "rigor" at all levels of schooling. The pressure is on for teachers to "get tough," "get efficient," "eliminate frills." Japanese schools are regularly held up as models of effectiveness, no doubt because Toyotas and Nissans are making life economically difficult for Chevys and Fords. Lee Iacocca, head of the Chrysler Corporation, is more widely respected for his views on education today than are the leaders of educational associations. Iacocca's notion of educational reform is to "knock some heads" to get teachers and students to shape up.

There is also enormous interest in such old/new ideas as:

- requiring a core curriculum so that students get more math, more science, more language, more history and social studies;
- increased standardized testing to ensure that students are learning more material; and
- a longer school year so that students have more time to study and learn all that "more."

However, as educator Charles McMurry has written, "We have already gone to the limit of filling up our curriculum with all kinds of information and many forms of activity" (*Teaching by Projects*. New York: Macmillan). And McMurry wrote that statement way back in 1924! If the curriculum was too full almost seventy years ago, what would McMurry think today?

Yet, in spite of this, one reform report after another today calls for additions — more lab work in science, new courses in computer literacy, more math courses, expanded foreign language study. Even if these additions are desirable, there's simply no place to put them, not on top of the schools' increasing responsibilities for surrogate parenting, sex education, and lunch, and certainly not in the face of more and more curricular time being consumed by standardized testing.

We know that knowledge is proliferating at an extraordinary rate. Research in all fields and disciplines is increasing knowledge by geometrical proportions, quickly clogging the lines of sophisticated computer networks designed to facilitate its flow. We already have an educational dilemma based solely on the quantity of knowledge that might need to be part of the school curriculum.

More important, I think, is the fact that we simply aren't reflecting enough on the quality and nature of the knowledge that should be offered in the schools. The knowledge demanded by the press and the public seems to be more of what students have never mastered in the first place — names and dates, facts and laws, landmarks in history, science, literature, math.

As an illustration of this rearview mirror-ism, take the National Geographic Society, which recently celebrated its hundredth anniversary by declaring war on "geographical illiteracy." Although the Society is sponsoring some interesting projects in hands-on geography, it has attracted most attention by sponsoring "geography bees" in which bright kids are quizzed on names and locations. I can't think of anything less likely to bring about geographical literacy than this sort of approach, which places a premium on memory and fails utterly to help youngsters make any connection between themselves and other people in other parts of the world.

The prospect of geography bees gave me a weird dream, one that (in theory, at least) could help solve the crisis in geography. I dreamt I was wearing a very large disk about my waist, made of chicken wire and held up by shoulder straps or suspenders so I could walk around with it. On the disk were painted the outlines of the continents. My body represented my home country, which gave me a good perspective on where I (literally) stood in relation to other lands. Then came the fun part. I had to hang my laundry out to dry on the disk, suspending each piece of clothing from the country where it was manufactured — Taiwan, Korea, Italy, France, etc.

I believe this dream is an effective demonstration that learning geography should be more than memorization. It needs to be a hands-on affair, where people see connections between their own interests (or socks) and distant regions of the globe.

The dominance of disciplinary learning

I want to seriously question the discipline-centered learning of our schools. By "discipline" here I simply mean any body of knowledge organized for instruction and research, such as math, chemistry, literature or social studies.

The disciplines help us create and organize knowledge, and they provide important ways of systematizing and sharing learning. Yet, as Colonel Francis Parker remarked in his *Talks on Pedagogics* in 1894, "There is no classification in nature." There are rocks and animals and stars, but it is human beings who decided to study those in separate fields called geology, biology, and astronomy.

For purposes of research and scholarship, those classifications work reasonably well, and part of their success stems from the fact that they allow people to specialize. Since nobody could ever know all there is to know about rocks and animals and stars, it makes sense to focus on a discipline. As knowledge proliferates, subdisciplines proliferate. One of my friends is a clay mineralogist whose geological specialty is varieties of soil; another is a micro-biologist who ignores lions and tigers to focus on the smaller critters that live inside them and you and me; a third is an ethno-musicologist who ignores Beethoven and Stravinsky to focus on folk music and its connection with culture.

But should that kind of thinking also apply to the young learner, the novice, the person who is not ready to write scholarly papers or probe the frontiers of learning?

For a long time educators have assumed that initial learning is best presented in disciplinary structures. We start with "the basics" of the discipline and work our way up to more complicated structures. From addition and subtraction we move on to calculus, from parts of speech to literature, from the periodic table to chemical equations, from historical chronology to social understanding. But is this truly the best way to present knowledge? I don't think so.

What I sense in this pattern is the imposition of a university model on schools: if only the schools would cover those nagging basics, then the universities could get on with teaching the advanced work. Colleges have already pushed their disciplinary focus down to high schools. University professors commonly complain that entering college students aren't prepared, so they have to teach courses introducing their disciplines, when they'd rather have the high schools do that. The disciplinary focus is less strong in middle schools and junior high schools, yet the unique feature of those levels is that students there get to change classes and meet specialized teachers — English, math, science. The elementary classroom generally remains under the control of a single teacher, yet even there we find an increasing emphasis on disciplinary knowledge, on subjects and textbooks, on fragmenting the self-contained classroom into instructional modules and periods, even on introducing disciplinary specialties earlier.

But what if students can't or won't or don't learn the disciplinary basics because they can't see the big picture?

Teaching more history, ironically and perhaps predictably, won't result in learning more history. Pushing more disciplinary science won't necessarily produce children who know more about science; in fact, it may even create children who simply don't like science. And one has only to look at mathematics and its headlines to see what teaching a discipline in isolation will do.

Nor will gimmicking up disciplinary learning with audio visuals and computers save the day, even though that might well be an improvement over standard textbooks.

Hands-on or "discovery" learning won't help either, if they are limited to pseudo-discovery of conventional disciplinary laws. True hands-on learning is highly desirable, but seldom are students actually allowed to figure things out for themselves. Many so-called discovery approaches simply turn textbook knowledge into a phony laboratory or question and answer session.

The interdisciplinary alternative

Although the idea of interdisciplinary studies isn't particularly new, it has received a strong push in our time through C.P. Snow's widely discussed book, *The Two Cultures* (Cambridge: Cambridge University Press, 1959). Snow was particularly concerned about a schism between science and the humanities. He wrote, "The number two is a very dangerous number," and he argued that humanities and science scholars have very little understanding of and respect for one another's work.

He might have added that, within those two communities, there are other bifurcations. Literary people and historians, for example, don't always talk to one another, and neither do chemists and biologists, or even "applied" linguists and "theoretical" linguists. He was right. The number two represents division, separation, isolation, and mutual ignorance.

Whatever the number of separate disciplines being taught, that number is also dangerous. Teaching — even in self-contained classrooms — is subdivided by disciplines from kindergarten to grade twelve, each field marching to its own drummer, each following its own internal logic. Fractions are taught the same year as South America; biological classification is taught the same month as the geography of the Pacific Rim. There is no integration, not even a rationale for teaching them at the same time.

This lack of coordination is, of course, wasteful of teaching energy. It also indirectly teaches a dangerous lesson. It impresses upon young learners a false vision of disciplinary independence. It effectively teaches them to make no connections whatever among the various parts of their study, to forget math once the social studies lesson begins, never to apply what they learned in language arts in their science class.

Snow argued that such a schism is more than wasteful; it may prove fatal to humankind. He believed that for the sake of humankind — quite literally its survival — the gap between the two cultures must be bridged. Remarkably, he wrote long before our current awareness of the greenhouse effect, acid rain, the depletion of the ozone layer, and the discovery of many side effects of pesticides, fertilizers, artificial dyes, preservatives, and so on.

Increasing numbers of teachers today share Snow's vision. In particular, I'm encouraged by new combined courses in science, technology, and society, which help elementary and secondary school students see some of the relationships between scientific discoveries, technological applications, and their anticipated and unanticipated effects on society.

Snow called for a bridging of only two cultures. The interdisciplinary alternative calls for the bridging of many. Fortunately, there are signs of increasing interest in this philosophy.

In the English language arts, for example, a movement for "language across the curriculum" has helped to show the importance of making connections by demonstrating that language is a fundamental part of all knowing and learning. A (newly formed) Assembly on Science and Humanities of the National Council of Teachers of English is committed to the broad principles of holistic interdisciplinary learning through language.

In history and social studies, teachers are interested in getting the past out of textbooks and into kids' hands through neighborhood history projects, study of real objects and artifacts, and original research, all teaching techniques which naturally cut across disciplinary boundaries. The National Association for Core Curriculum is one focal point for such activities. (See pages 61-63 for a list of other teaching organizations that share a concern for interdisciplinary studies.) And the American Association for the Advancement of Science has recently and radically declared that science must be taught as a liberal art, with study organized around topics or themes rather than following strictly disciplinary lines (*The Chronicle of Higher Education*, 5/9/90, A1, A16).

Let me be quick to add that I don't see interdisciplinary learning as a cure-all, a total solution to all curriculum problems. It isn't even a uniform program or set of concepts. However, interdisciplinary learning holds out great promise for improved — even joyful — learning, and it offers a true and attractive alternative to many of the non-reforms of disciplinary learning currently being proposed.

What is interdisciplinarity?

Interdisciplinarity can be as simple as a first-grader doing a science/social studies project on volcanoes, or it can be as dervishly complex as taking a bunch of seventh-graders to nature camp for a weekend. It can involve well-organized groups of faculty members orchestrating their teaching around themes, but it can also be a single teacher who approaches traditional textbook learning with an interdisciplinary perspective.

Interdisciplinarity is, as William Mayville has titled his book on the topic, *The Mutable Paradigm* (Washington: American Association for Higher Education, 1978).

We needn't haggle over precise definitions. In his book, Mayville discusses fine distinctions between such terms as multi-disciplinarity (where different disciplines — for example, music, math, and history — work together), pluri-disciplinarity (where related fields — for example, math and physics — work together), and trans-disciplinarity (where disciplines find a common set of operating principles). For our purposes, interdisciplinarity involves looking at issues, problems, school content, and the world as a whole from many different perspectives, without a great deal of worry about whether, at any given moment, students are studying math or history or science or, ideally, all elements of the curriculum in concert.

Perhaps most commonly, interdisciplinary learning is centered on themes or topics rather than on specific facts or concepts from within a discipline. It is generally focused on something of interest or importance in the real world, with the reality of that world often being driven by young learners' interests and needs. The following list provides an "alphabet" of representative topics for interdisciplinary study.

An alphabet of interdisciplinary themes and topics

aborigines	jokes	questions
bicycles	kinesics (body talk)	rebels
cities	locks	space
dinosaurs	machines	technology
energy	maps	utopias
families	myths	vegetables
flight	noise	war and peace
garbage	ozone	xenophobia
heroes/heroines	pseudo-science	youth and age
inventions	quarks	zoos

I've found that most of these topics interest students from kindergarten through college, though some are clearly better suited to younger learners than older. To illustrate their interdisciplinarity, consider possible classroom explorations of:

Bicycles

The math and mechanics of their construction, the physics of balancing one, their history, their future, the geography of bike tripping, poems and songs about bikes. You can even build one out of spare parts.

Classics

Students answer questions like, "What makes a 'classic' car, fairy tale, popular song, film, television program?" (Two kids in a second-language class have assured me that Michael J. Fox is a classic actor because his movies will endure forever. They had the definition of a classic right, at least!)

Questions

The ultimate interdisciplinary unit, in which students pose questions about what they think really matters and pursue answers in many different fields and disciplines.

We sometimes think of disciplines in a limited way — math and physics and history and English. I've included another of my alphabets, one that helps us think more broadly. This one shows just a few of hundreds of fields and disciplines that can provide a focus for integrated studies. (Remember that I use "field" and "discipline" to stand for any area where people systematically collect knowledge.) You can probably add dozens more without thinking too hard about it.

An alphabet of fields and disciplines

agriculture	foreign languages	optics
algebra	forensics	optometry
anatomy	forestry	ornithology
anthropology	genealogy	orthopedics
architecture	genetics	osteopathy
art	geometry	pediatrics
auto mechanics	health	philosophy
biology	heraldry	photography
botany	history	poetics
calculus	ichthyology	popular culture
cartography	judicial studies	psychology
chemistry	junk food studies**	pyrotechnics
child development	kinetics	radiology
chiropractics	law	reading
cinematography	linguistics	rhetoric
communication	medicine	scientology
computer science	metallurgy	social science
dance	meteorology	theology
dentistry	military science	trigonometry
dodoism*	mime	UFO studies
drama	mineralogy	umbilical cord studies
ecology	music	vegetarianism
economics	mythology	weather
electricity	natural science	women's studies
entomology	neurology	xerography
ethnography	numismatics	x-ray technology
folklore	nursing	yoga
food science	occult science	zoology

* I made up "dodoism." I define it as the study either of dumb ideas or of ideas that have faded into extinction (like a balanced budget).

** There is, after all, a Hamburger University run by McDonald's.

I find it interesting to choose a topic from the themes and topics list and, off the cuff, see how the fields and disciplines in this list can be brought to bear on it. Given, say, a unit of study on the lowly vegetable, what new ideas and information might be brought in if you cross-referenced it with such fields as art (can we look for examples of vegetables in art?), electricity (have you seen one of those science kits which uses a potato to power an electric clock?), geometry (let's cut open an avocado and examine its symmetry), or rhetoric (how do parents persuade their kids to eat their veggies?)?

I don't mean to suggest that learners should be put through the misery of checking off every field or discipline in this list to see whether or not it has been covered. In fact, for the elementary grades, I don't think it's particularly helpful for students to worry about the names of disciplines at all (though they might have some fun quizzing their parents on fields like ichthyology and numismatics). Rather, I simply want to show that thinking in an interdisciplinary way forces us — teachers and students — to take new angles of vision on our studies.

The aims of interdisciplinary study

In his book *Basic Skills* (Little, Brown, 1982), Herbert Kohl argued for six basic skills which children need to develop "if they are to learn how to function effectively and compassionately as adults" (pp. 110-111):

1. The ability to use language well and thoughtfully.

2. The ability to think through a problem and experiment with solutions.

3. The ability to use scientific and technological ideas and to use tools.

4. The ability to use the imagination.

5. The ability to understand how people function in groups.

6. The ability to know how to learn something yourself.

His list encompasses the "big four" of school disciplines: English (1, 2), math (2, 3) science (2, 3), and history/social studies (5), as well as critical and imaginative thinking (2, 4, 6).

To this, any advocate of interdisciplinary learning says, simply: "Admirable, but why not teach these six basics together?" So much of learning invites children and adults to integrate skills and knowledge. As learners of all ages puzzle over, say, problems of aging, or the ecology of a pond, or the arrival of spring, or the creation of a family tree, they draw concurrently on skills of number, language, scientific inquiry, social studies, and imaginative and critical thinking.

Some principles of interdisciplinary learning

Before going on to show some examples of interdisciplinary projects, I want to present here what I see as the central principles — the claims — of interdisciplinary learning.

- Learning must be linked to students' concerns, values, and questions; it cannot simply be centered around the structures of disciplines.

- Disciplinary and interdisciplinary knowledge is not random or unstructured; at best, it meshes with young people's interests by helping them understand their world.

- Learning through questioning, firsthand experience, and experimentation creates more complete mastery then does passive reception of information through texts, lectures, or even audio-visual presentations.

- Linking learning across disciplines and subject areas leads to greater learning than teaching the discipline in isolation.

- Interdisciplinary learning can be pursued in subject-centered classes (for example, math, science, history) at virtually any time.

- Interdisciplinary inquiry is open-ended and intellectually engaging for learners of all ages.

An interdisciplinary sampler

The world does not present itself to us in a naturally standardized fashion. There can therefore be no standardized look to interdisciplinary units, classes, courses, or curricula. The following examples of interdisciplinary teaching and learning merely represent the range and breadth of possibilities — and I both acknowledge and warn that they show just the tip of the iceberg. ("Iceberg" is an apt metaphor here, but it's also a potential topic for study.)

The "project" approach

In the previous chapter I referred to Charles McMurry and his remarkable 1924 book *Teaching by Projects*. McMurry was a "progressive" educator in the original sense of the term: a participant in the movement toward experiential learning created by John Dewey. "Projects" — interdisciplinary theme or topic units — were common in U.S. schools in the 1920s and 1930s. As McMurry pointed out, they could be done individually at home (a bird house, a rabbit trap, a homemade telephone) or be school based (the invention of the cotton gin, the planning of a canal lock, or Robinson Crusoe's projects of cave-making, boat-building, and taming of animals — p. 1). Projects could naturally emerge from art, agriculture, geography, science, history, biography, literature, or any other elementary or secondary school subject.

He argued that project teaching allowed teachers to organize learning into wholes, focus teaching on productive ends, improve efficiency of instruction, teach practical applications, and capture the energy of young learners.

Some of the specific school projects in the book took "hands on learning" literally. McMurry described a school garden project where youngsters researched growing food as they plotted and laid out a garden, then seeded, watered, weeded, and harvested it. Such a project would draw on science, mathematics, language, and the school of hard knocks. Other manual projects he proposed included concreting a basement floor, papering and decorating a family living room, constructing a corn crib, and — still leaving kids a bit of play — building a tree house (p. 20). Clearly these kinds of projects were naturals in rural school systems where children were expected to learn the skills of farming and home maintenance.

In a more academic vein, McMurry reported on projects developed through the educational program at George Peabody College. In them, elementary and secondary students researched the development and architecture of

Washington D.C.; mapped, read and wrote about an overland trip to California in 1848; and investigated a U.S. Government irrigation project.

For each of these projects (and many others described in the book), he listed three principles (pp. 84-88):

- An "inductive-deductive thought-movement" in which youngsters puzzled over their own questions, sought answers, and tested applications.

- "Progressive assimilation and use of new knowledge," where students actively synthesized ideas across disciplines and designed solutions to problems they had identified.

- "Self-activity in the independent and reflective use of knowledge," so that through engagement in whole class projects, children found individual areas of interest and expertise.

This kind of project teaching isn't widely known, which is why I mention it at some length. In many respects, McMurry was more than seventy years ahead of his time. As you'll see, much present-day interdisciplinary teaching follows very closely the philosophy and methods of the early project teachers.

Given the widespread and sometimes irresponsible criticism of schools these days, we should heed McMurry's rational voice objecting to the narrowness of traditional, discipline-centered, school studies: "They lack stimulus and free scope. They cramp and hinder spontaneous movement in what might be a rich, growing field of thought. Freedom to think out problems is impossible within such narrow boundaries, just as freedom and flexibility of speech are denied to one who is narrowly limited in vocabulary." (pp. 93-94).

We could do worse than to follow McMurry's lead even today and adopt project approaches. I'm not saying, however, that everything there is to know about interdisciplinary teaching was discovered by 1924. I'm convinced we can build on those early experiences to do even better today.

Teaching by topics

An approach to learning similar to McMurry's was developed and tested in British infant schools in the 1930s, and many U.K. primary schools still follow those footsteps. This model also selects themes or "topics" to unify children's study. One of the best known teachers in this model is Sybil Marshall, who described her work in *An Experiment in Education* (Cambridge and New York: Cambridge University Press, 1963).

Marshall used art as a means of opening up children's minds to experiences, and she used children's artwork as a way of unifying the entire curriculum. She taught in a primary school in Cambridgeshire, which served the small working class community of Kingston. "The school was the ugliest building in the place, and even that was mellowed by a hundred years of wear and tear, and by the ivy which covered a host of architectural and structural defects." (p. 27).

Encountering bored and listless students, and saddled with a syllabus calling for the study of Rome, Ms. Marshall launched a project to write "The Book of Kingston," tracing the village back to its roots, including the Roman occupation of England. She would write the following message on the board (p. 49):

GONE PAINTING. FIND US IN THE FIELD
BEHIND THE CONGREGATIONAL CHAPEL

and the children would go outside the school for their learning. They visited historic sites in the area and sifted through community record fragments, recording what they saw in writing and artwork. While discovering their own history and traditions, they moved from art into music, dance, arithmetic and science. One of the most spectacular activities reported in the book was a scale topographical map of old Kingston that the students created on the school playground. Just think of the range of skills and disciplines that would be drawn into the execution of such a project.

Teaching by topics became quite popular in England, Australia, and New Zealand in the 1960s. Geoffrey Summerfield's book *Topics in English* (London: Batsford, 1965) describes work which naturally cuts across disciplinary lines, as students explore "Predators . . . Australia . . . Fire and Flame . . . Snakes and Reptiles . . . Old Age . . . Hunting . . . Sky Journeys . . ." and others. Under Summerfield's scheme, students would read fiction, nonfiction, and poetry about a particular topic, then engage in a variety of reading, research, and imaginative projects. For snakes and reptiles, for example, their work might vary from scientific study of a snake kept in a classroom vivarium to imaginative writing about snakes in a jungle setting. I encountered Summerfield's book early in my teaching career, and it changed my teaching irrevocably.

The topics approach is applicable in many subject areas. For instance, Owen Craddy's *Topics in Mathematics* (same year and publisher as Summerfield's book) showed how students could be drawn into math study through such different projects as computing the probability of winning a football pool and learning how to navigate around the world.

Since those promising days, the popularity of topical teaching has waned. One problem has been teacher uncertainty about whether or not basic skills were being adequately covered. A more common complaint has been that teachers settle into a rut, teaching the same topics year after year, just as they might work through the same textbook year after year.

It's easy to see how this might happen, especially if teachers pay more attention to their need for control than to the inventive contributions their students can make to the topic. To me, its changing nature is precisely one of the most joyful aspects of interdisciplinary, project-oriented teaching. No teacher needs to get stuck or become bored, for even if one does the same general topic, say navigation, for a few years in a row, different children will try to take that topic in different directions — one year to the South Seas, the next to outer space, the following year to exploring their own neighborhood . . . The trick is to follow the lead of the children.

People and their environment

I now offer you a recent example of interdisciplinary teaching drawn from my own work with undergraduate prospective teachers. This unit illustrated the full range and scope of interdisciplinary teaching. The number of participants was larger than would normally be the case in an individual school's project, but I see no reason why a classroom teacher could not do the same kind of thing.

This project involved thirty undergraduates who were taking an interdisciplinary learning course, eighty middle school students who were part of an interdisciplinary biology/language arts/social studies team, and the staff of the university museum. My students prepared original instructional materials, introduced the middle graders to them, guided the kids on a field trip to the museum, and conducted follow-up sessions.

The unit theme was "people and their environment." I chose it because it was extraordinarily broad and would offer points of interest for virtually any student or teacher.

I began by meeting with the middle school teachers and the education directors of the museum to work out a timetable. Then I introduced the topic to my students and had them brainstorm for subtopics. What might be useful for middle schoolers to study about their engagement with the environment? Out of our charting, mapping, and discussion, seven subtopics emerged, each with a team of three to five undergraduates to work on it:

- Exploration/exploitation of natural resources
- Interaction of colonists and first Americans
- Adaptation for survival
- Religion and culture
- Health issues
- The climate
- Tools and technology

Obviously other important subtopics might have emerged, but these were the choices of my undergraduate students. They took care to leave ample room for the middle schoolers to develop their own stake in the topics. In fact, the subtopics were still fairly broad.

Prior to our first visit to the middle school, my undergraduates collected materials on the topics — magazine articles, short stories and poetry, music and art. They also visited the university museum and borrowed some artifacts to take with them to the school. During this research time, a panel of the middle schoolers visited my class to give us all the lowdown on what kids "that age" are like.

Our next step was to send descriptions — advertisements really — of the subtopics over to the school. The middle schoolers used the descriptions to form themselves into groups, with some guidance from their teachers.

During our first meeting at the middle school, my students introduced the topics by means of some hands on inquiry learning. The "survival" subgroup got the students to play a game that required thought about the tools and supplies they would need to survive in an alien environment. The "tools" group brought in some nineteenth century tools from the museum and had the kids guess their function and manufacture. The "health" group began by having the youngsters think of family and folk cures for common ailments — coughs, cinder in the eye, hiccups — and raise questions about the scientific sources of those ideas.

After the introduction of the subtopics, the middle school students were given a chance to raise their own questions about them. They readily volunteered:

- What's going to happen with the greenhouse effect?
- How do people with different religious systems differ in living styles?
- What happened to the Indians as a result of colonization in the U.S.?

During the following week, the two groups of students together visited the museum to look for answers. Instead of scurrying about filling in answers on worksheets, the middle schoolers, with help from my students, combed the exhibits searching for answers to their own questions. From time to time the groups would take a break, assemble in a classroom, and write about what they were seeing and learning. The museum educators were especially pleased, because in contrast to many school tours, our gang knew what they wanted to learn, focused on the exhibits, and went away with a deepened understanding of people and their environment.

We wrapped up the unit a week later by having the two groups of students together discuss the questions they had raised and demonstrate the learning they had done. The health group focused on what youngsters can do to preserve their own health. They included a step-test of heart rates for the rest of the students. Those interested in tools wrote science fiction proposals for tools of the future. The religion/culture group synthesized its findings by developing a concept map of world religions. Each of the groups also brainstormed for interdisciplinary extensions for their topic — ideas about what individuals or groups could do to learn more about the topic or to take action in their own lives.

Learning something new

In another unit I teach with college students, I follow a very different pattern. I tell them simply: "Learn something new." My students have learned to cross country ski, juggle, play the harmonica, bake (males), tune an automobile engine (females), knit (males and females), do judo, do karate, meditate, draw, cartoon, do calligraphy, play guitar, play accordion, and so on.

When I launch the unit, I first review some of the basic ways in which people — all of us — learn: trial and error, messing around, reading a book, taking lessons, talking with people who know. I then urge my students to try any or all of these approaches to learn a new skill, any way they can.

I have the students maintain a journal or log of their learning experience, keeping special note of how they seem to learn most successfully, where they run into blocks, how they achieve breakthroughs. We conclude the unit by sharing our newly acquired skills — actually teaching them to one another. Students tell me this is one of the units they find most valuable in my course, not only for the new skills they acquire, but for the deepened understanding of their own learning.

In what sense is this project an interdisciplinary one? I suppose I should rather say that it's non-disciplinary or trans-disciplinary. The object is to learn a skill by any means possible, which erases traditional disciplinary boundaries. But my students and I also discover that traditional disciplines help us in our learning. There is math involved in learning to play the harmonica, science (and psychology) in knowing how to control a pair of skis, history in mastering almost any skill. And language and literacy are involved universally, whether we read a book or simply talk to a friend who knows how to do what we want to learn.

In the not-so-bleak midwinter

Interdisciplinary learning can be done by teachers and children at any grade level. One of the most comprehensive interdisciplinary units I've ever seen was prepared by three kindergarten teachers at the American School in Taipei.

Karen Kirk, Virginia Rogers, and Clarene Tossey chose the theme of winter for a topic. I offered my professorial observation that sub-tropical Taiwan doesn't have a traditional North American winter, but they pointed out that winter is a global topic and can be usefully employed for a rich variety of explorations. Actually, they explained, it does sometimes snow in the mountains north of Taipei, and a great number of Taipei people rush out to observe that rare Taiwanese commodity.

They sketched out a calendar for what they called a "metaphorical month" of winter activities, a crowded calendar that could realistically occupy several months to do it full justice. (That is a common happening in interdisciplinary teaching. What starts out as a core topic often unfolds and extends in many directions. Although one isn't obliged to follow every idea, trail, hint, suggestion, possibility, or question that emerges, interdisciplinary teaching temptingly interconnects the world for us and makes it difficult to draw boundaries.)

The Taipei winter calendar they created is shown on the following page. Down the left-hand column are listed some of the disciplines which are covered in this unit for kindergartners, a list that includes, for instance, art, mathematics, computers, music, reading, and social studies. Each daily "lesson" is based on a single question, one raised by the children themselves. These questions are explored through discussion, art, dramatic play, improvisation, media, and hands-on experimentation and craft work. The children make maps and study globes, create snowflake art, make snow, pour maple syrup on snow to make "ice cream," write stories, sing songs . . . Virtually every lesson also draws on a work of children's literature, either fiction or nonfiction. The far right-hand column shows some of the outside-of-school experiences that connect with the unit as well.

Topics and Disciplines	MONDAY	TUESDAY	WEDNESDAY	THURSDAY	FRIDAY	Field Trips and Other Resources
"Winter Season" Science Geography Math Literature Art Music Computers	"Why does it snow?" Filmstrip: "The Changing Seasons" Lit: A Book of Seasons and The Season Collection	"Where does snow come from?" Field trip: Weather station Photo display of winter photographs.	"Where does it snow?" Class discussion and roleplaying. Journal writing and illustrations.	"What do snowflakes look like?" Drama: Roleplay Art: Cutting snowflakes	"What happens when snow melts?" Sequence lesson, cutting and pasting. Sing: "Frosty" Computer: Melting snowman	Weather station Snowman video Science teacher Encyclopedia Filmstrips Globe and maps Childcraft materials
"Animals in Winter" Literature Art Math Dramatic Play	"What animals like the snow?" Read "The Rabbit and the Turnip" (Chinese fairy tale) Lit: The Big Snow	"What happens to animals in winter?" School science teacher will discuss colors, hibernation, etc. Lit: The Snow Parade	"How do animals protect themselves?" Film on animal survival. Game: Survival in wintertime	"How do Taiwanese farmers protect their animals?" Field trip: Taipei farm. Lit: Winter Magic	"How can people help animals?" Craft: Make bird-feeder Lit: Deer in the Snow	Farm field trip Science teacher Videos National Geographic video: Bears
"People in Winter" Social Studies Art Health Math Literature	"What do people wear in winter?" Filmstrip: "Winter on the Farm" Photos: Winter wear Lit: White Snow	"How do you dress when it snows?" Bring in family photos from U.S. Lit: Over the River and Through the Wds.	"Where do people live in winter?" Lit: The Little Igloo	"Why do people get colds in winter?" School nurse discusses health care. Lit: The Winter Noisy Books	"What do people eat in winter?" Cook: Chicken soup with rice, cocoa Lit: Sugar on Snow, Chicken Soup with Rice	School nurse Parents Film Audio cassettes Childraft materials Library books
"Winter Activities" Sports Music Dance Astronomy Computers Social Studies Art	Lit: The Day Daddy Stayed Home	"How do people get around in winter?" Bring in snowshoes. Crafts: Make snowshoes. Lit: Cross Country Cat	"What do the stars look like?" Field trip: Observatory, winter sky. Lit: Mole's Family Christmas	"What are some good winter sports?" Video: Winter sports Computer game: Olympics	"What can you do at home in a snow-storm?" Popcorn plus journal writing. Lit: Popcorn Book	Outdoorsman P.E. teacher Observatory Videos Maps Parent helpers Library books
"Winter Holidays" Social Studies Geography Music Dance Drama Arts and Crafts	"How do people celebrate?" Swedish mother to visit class. Lit: Holly and Ivy	"How can we help?" Crafts: Making gifts. Clustering: Ways to help out.	"What are special holiday foods?" Jewish mother talks of Hannukah Poem: "Eight Days"	"What are family traditions?" German mother discusses. Lit: Night Before...	"How do you get ready for a party?" Set up for class party. Program for parents. Visit from St. Nick	St. Nick Home ec. teacher Parents Music teacher

As exhaustive as the unit is, it's only one of four seasonal units that Karen, Virginia, and Clarene are planning for their youngsters. One might worry that a curriculum based solely on the seasons could become one-dimensional. However, the richness of their outline demonstrates that such a topic, like many others, unfolds in so many directions that boredom or saturation seems a small danger.

The elemental universe

In a deliberate effort to test the limits (or nonlimits) of interdisciplinary study, I once selected the unlikely topic of the old Greek partition of the elements for a middle school interdisciplinary exploration. In a primitive early version of atomic theory, some Greek philosophers claimed that everything on earth was made of four basic elements: air, earth, water, and fire. Within those four topics, my middle schoolers could explore just about any question that was of interest to them.

The unit opened with a display of books from the middle school library — fiction and nonfiction titles ranging from energy to firefighting (fire), farming to geography (earth), pollution to flight (air), and hydraulics to deserts (water). After reading, thinking, and discussing, students identified areas they wanted to learn more about. As well as learning from books, they were encouraged (but not required) to look for other resources within reach. For example, they could make visits to local businesses and institutions (the power generating facility, the local history museum), or talk with people who might help them, in person or by telephone.

The middle schoolers proved me (and possibly the Greeks) right, for they covered everything under, on and beyond the sun. Our final show'n'tell day included a demonstration of a model solar swimming pool heater (fire), a drama simulating life in outer space (earth and air), marigolds grown in a variety of soils (earth), seafood cookies (water), and research into the Greenpeace movement (which its researcher classified as helping to save air, earth and water).

The Bongo program

One of the most exciting and comprehensive interdisciplinary programs is simply called "Bongo." As it exists, Bongo is for high school students, but the heart of it is easily adaptable to both lower and higher levels. Its creators, Terry Born and Paul Jablon of Middle College High School in Long Island City, New York, don't explain the name, but they have written in detail about how they run the program (*The Bongo Workbook*. The ECHO Project, La Guardia Community College, 1987.)

Bongo is team taught and project centered. Themes have included "evolution and revolution," "the rights of individuals vs. the rights of society," and "utopias." The evolution-revolution unit included work in science (fossils, the origins of earth, the Bible and evolution), psychology (stages of development), art (from medieval to pop), English (from Ovid's *Metamorphoses* to *Kiss of the Spider Woman* by Manuel Puig), and oral communication (improvisation, persuasive speaking, debate).

The program has a strong focus on theater, and virtually every Bongo project ends with a public presentation to the whole school, usually a scripted play or docu-drama which lays out issues, problems, and an agenda for action. The Bongo teachers also believe in the Greek notion of a sound mind in a sound body. Students who elect the program sign a contract to jog specified distances every week.

Learning in the "real world"

A teacher once challenged me at an in-service meeting when I used the phrase "real world" to describe what goes on outside the classroom. "School is the real world," he contended, "and we should never dismiss the classroom as being somehow false or irrelevant."

I granted his point, though I still maintain that in practice there is too often an enormous gap between what youngsters do in school and what they see happening in the world around them. In my experience, most teachers agree that we need to make more explicit the ties between world happenings and phenomena and what we teach in our classrooms. Two books have been especially helpful to me in making this "real world" connection.

The Yellow Pages of Learning Resources, edited by Saul Wurman, was published way back in 1972 (Washington, D.C.: National Association of Secondary School Principals). Based on the Philadelphia Parkway School Project, a "school without walls," this book presented community-based projects — from A to Z — in a facsimile of the telephone yellow pages. It reviewed what kids could learn at an airport, a bakery, a car dealership, and so forth. Wurman made the point that schools could make fuller use of community resources than they do, whether the school is located in a large or small town.

That the book is now out of print doesn't matter, for any set of telephone yellow pages will work the same way. When students are engaged in projects, you simply have them flip through the directory seeking local businesses, industries, service organizations, and institutions which might have answers for their questions. Students can then either make appointments and visit those places — individually or as a class — or use the telephone itself as a tool for inquiry.

As I noted above, while working on the air/earth/water/fire project, my middle schoolers were encouraged to draw on area resources. They found help in places that ranged from a local health food store (a source of recipes and supplies for seaweed cookies) to an automobile assembly plant (for information on whatever happened to Oldsmobile's "rocket" engine).

In *City as Classroom* (Agincourt, Ontario: Book Society of Canada, Ltd., 1977), Marshall McLuhan, Eric McLuhan, and Katherine Hutcheon offered strategies for having classrooms investigate the world. In typical McLuhan fashion, they focused on the impact of various technologies (or media), including money, television, automobiles, lighting, and computers. They suggested gathering data — observing your world — and interpreting it by making sense of what you see.

One of my former students has reminded me of an adaptation I once made to this approach. She and several classmates spent a rainy afternoon counting cars and timing the stoplight intervals at a congested intersection in town. As part of my English class I had assigned students to investigate a local issue or problem before writing to people in authority about it. They were preparing recommendations to send to city council, an exercise which obviously involved a great deal of scientific measurement, mathematics, and logical interpretation, as well as English.

Wrongheaded ideas

My final example of interdisciplinary teaching focuses on a kind of anti-learning or anti-truth. In his *Directory of Discarded Ideas* (Sevenoaks, U.K.: Ashgrove, 1971), John Grant observes that many ideas and concepts that are now regarded as eccentric or crackpot were taken utterly seriously at one time. He invites us to explore obsolete or discredited ideas and theories "to show how empty and inaccurate Man's smug 'knowledge' has been."

Grant notes, for example, that the philosopher Hegel informed the world in 1800 that no objects in the solar system remained to be discovered, that Charles Darwin offered innumerable wrong theories before he hit it right with evolution, and that Thomas Aquinas declared that one of the things God couldn't do was draw a triangle with more or fewer than 180 degrees, "yet this is something which we can all do, by the simple expedient of drawing the triangle on a curved surface" (p. 3). Grant's book (and there are similarly irreverent books in most libraries) looks at fascinating failed ideas that range from belief in a hollow earth, to N-rays ("scientifically proven" from inaccurate data), to commonly known archaeological frauds such as Piltdown Man.

Borrowing directly from Grant's "Do-It-Yourself Dud Theory Kit," I have asked my students to create false beliefs and theories. Grant explains (p. 236):

There is nothing more enjoyable than spending a Sunday afternoon devising a really watertight odd theory . . . and it is alarming how easy it is to do. So I'd like you to take this opportunity to join me in my little hobby. Put aside your crossword (or even this book), draw together a few facts, think of the most ludicrous linking explanation for them, and then see how many other relevant facts or factoids you can fit into the structure.

In my version, I ask students to put together evidence to prove the "theory" that the earth is flat. My purpose is not to undo their previous schooling, but to get them to question what passes for conventional wisdom in their textbooks. Much of the sensory data we receive indicates that the world is flat (or at least that it's not a ball).

Students of all ages delight in developing quite sophisticated interdisciplinary theories and explanations to disprove widely accepted theories. I have also invited them to disprove all of the following:

- The universe is made of tiny particles called atoms.
- We breathe in oxygen and exhale carbon dioxide.
- The sun is the center of our solar system.
- Things fall because of gravity.
- Vegetables are good for you.

They also have a good time developing and proving fantastic ideas such as:

- The devil made me do it.
- School makes people dumber.
- Our school is shifting ground.
- You can analyze a person's character from his/her height.

Our aim in this type of work is not to support misstatements and false ideas — of course not. Rather, the exercise gets at the heart of all of interdisciplinary learning. It develops students who have a questioning frame of mind, who are interested in seeking a broad range of solutions to issues and problems, and who can range freely across disciplinary boundaries in search of knowledge and understanding.

Planning for interdisciplinary teaching

Futurescapes and realities

The time

Somewhere in the imaginable future, when humankind has figured out what to do with the trash, what to do about the ozone, how to share more equally with one's neighbor.

The place

They used to call it "school." The "schoolhouse" resembles a late twentieth century shopping mall, with numerous rooms filled with glittery intellectual attractions, opening into a nicely landscaped courtyard area where youngsters gather to eat, read, write, talk. Within the rooms — or intellectual boutiques — are the tools of learning. One contains computers which are networked to various information and data bases around the world; another contains microscopes and telescopes (the latter poking through observatory windows in the roof); a third contains recent magazines and newspapers; a fourth, current and useful videos; still others contain individual workstations (which they used to call desks), one per student, each station linked to a central computer.

The curriculum

Fully interdisciplinary, centered on topics negotiated among the students, faculty, and parents. This year the school is focusing attention on "cultural basics," exploring how various people on earth have developed customs, lifestyles, technologies, literatures, and arts to reflect their own perception of the world in which they live.

- Elementary school children are emphasizing poetry, music, legend, dance, and lifestyles.

- Middle schoolers are studying coming of age in many societies; they are corresponding with kids in other lands in Esperanto, the international language, via computer.

- Senior high students are studying politics, economics, literature, and science/technology.

For all levels, the year's study will end with a series of displays, presentations, student-produced films, and dramas in an international cultural festival.

The teachers

Liberally educated people who enjoy introducing kids to new ideas. Many of them travel during their non-teaching time. In addition to their general education, deliberately multidisciplinary, each has developed a specialty in a single discipline. The teachers work comfortably together on interdisciplinary teams, with teachers of science, mathematics, language, and social studies each lending specific expertise as students explore and solve problems. In addition, the faculty members have an extraordinary number of hobbies — from classic cars to cycling to quilting — hobbies which they pursue, among other times, during regularly scheduled "exploration days" at the school.

Okay. Enough of the daydream. Now back to reality.

But what reality? The promising thing is that all of the elements in my futurescape exist in one form or another already in some of today's schools. And so does the potential for interdisciplinary study.

Isaac Asimov once remarked that science fiction doesn't so much create new worlds as extend the present one. Teachers don't have to wait until the twenty-first or thirty-first century to implement the ideals, visions, and dreams of interdisciplinary teaching. What one can imagine, one can pursue.

The kind of instruction I am describing in this book can be undertaken now, in today's schools, even with less-than-ideal resources, less-than-ideal facilities, less-than-ideal cooperation among faculty. Later in this chapter I'll discuss some planning and implementation possibilities for interdisciplinary teaching which I know from experience and observation can work *today*.

But first I want to describe several models for planning interdisciplinary units. They may seem too complex and time consuming, but I'll also show how these various planning procedures can be implemented in smaller bits, as small, perhaps, as a single class session, or even smaller, a ten minute mini-lesson. But I think it's important to begin with the full picture, then focus on what can be done within the limits of one's present classroom frame.

The Quest model

"Quest" is what I call the model that I use in my own interdisciplinary teaching. I've used it with whole classes of students and as a pattern for individual inquiry. It's a pattern I employ even in my own research. The Quest model can serve as an approach for faculty planning and collecting materials for interdisciplinary units, but it can also be a guide for youngsters who are essentially following their own (guided) path to knowledge.

This model has five stages:

- choosing a topic for exploration
- developing good questions
- finding resources
- conducting research
- synthesizing and sharing knowledge

1. Choosing a topic

On page 17 I provided an alphabet of interdisciplinary topics, but just about any topic, subject, or idea can lend itself to Quest. My favorite source of topics is the daily newspaper, and one activity I use with teachers and students is to take a newspaper — any newspaper, this morning's newspaper — and comb it for topics that raise interesting questions, that arouse curiosity.

Just for fun, I picked up a newspaper the morning I wrote this sentence and set myself a goal of finding fifty good topics for interdisciplinary investigation. The list below shows the results of my research.

Topics from the newspaper

Topic	Source
the Cold War	front page
cosmic radiation	front page
wagering and "fixes"	front page
memorials to heroes/heroines	front page
space travel	front page
government bureaucracy	front page
the weather	page two
segregation and apartheid	world news
freak accidents	filler
recycling (garbage-eating worms)	filler
terrorism	world news
democracy worldwide	world news
high achieving students	advertisement
food prices	advertisement
the Cold War (again)	editorial cartoon
conflicts of interest	editorial
newspaper coverage	letter to the editor
equal rights for all	letter to the editor
modern-day spies	column
tobacco selling	column
men and women	column

Russia	world news
Korea	world news
Panama	world news
Ireland	world news
labor-saving devices	advertisement
(electronic pencil sharpener)	
photography and videos	advertisement
"petworking"	feature
(matching pets with good owners)	
local crimes	"databank" page
flashy cars	feature
animal abuse	feature
(see also "petworking")	
earth's resources	feature
self-help	feature
drug abuse	feature
sleep and dreams	feature
recycling	feature
hit movies	feature
anti-smoking campaigns	feature
(see also "tobacco selling")	
rust and decay	feature
running, jogging, marathons	advertisement
music television	feature
computers	advertisement
electronic toys	advertisement
child movie stars	entertainment
embarrassment	Ann Landers
TV commercials	Erma Bombeck
health for young people	meeting announcement
acne cures	science
weight loss	advertisement
horoscopes	horoscope page

I reached fifty topics with ease, and I didn't get to the sports page, the current television listings, the comics page, the classifieds, or the crossword puzzle. (The crossword alone is often good for at least twenty-five ideas.) Obviously not every one of these topics is appropriate for school study. But I'll wager (see topic 3) that almost any group of children, young adults, or adults would find something they could use on the list. And tomorrow's newspaper will contain an equally fascinating set of possibilities.

I also scan the subject catalog in the library for possible topics, or simply browse the library, starting with the display of recently acquired books and winding up at the sections for children and young adults.

Of course, not all interdisciplinary teaching must or should begin with such an open list of topics. Teachers often have to take into account the prescribed curriculum and a list of concepts. But for them, the textbook can often provide ideas. Virtually any textbook chapter title will provide a topic for a lesson or unit, whether you're discussing volcanoes, simple machines, Peru, or prehistoric peoples. In fact, interdisciplinary teaching provides an easy way for the teacher to move beyond the often pedestrian presentation of a textbook to engage students deeply in study of a topic from multiple perspectives.

2. Developing questions

Interdisciplinary study is inextricably tied to inquiry learning, where students seek answers to questions which they see as important. And given an opportunity to raise questions and a degree of autonomy in setting priorities, kids do raise significant questions.

At a meeting of the National Association for Science, Technology, and Society, I was inspired by a high school math teacher from Denver, Colorado, who told of taking his senior high students to McDonald's, buying them burgers and fries, and asking them what topics they thought a good high school curriculum should cover. The issues they listed included communications, aging, the future of the planet, and human relationships. The teacher then went on to show that he could teach just about any math skill he wanted — and a good deal more than math — under the rubric of those questions.

Those were not "gifted" students, or a select group. When given an honest chance to explore and shown that their ideas are valued, any group of youngsters, from kindergarten on up, will raise significant and valuable issues.

Webbing and brainstorming

Teachers all over the globe seem to have discovered webbing as a good way to get students to generate questions for explorations. A main topic is written in the center of a large sheet of chart paper, on an overhead transparency, or on the chalkboard, then youngsters are invited to web outward, linking ideas. I like to do my webs on large poster boards or sheets of butcher paper, over several days so that the web can grow and become more intricate. On the next page is a sample brainstorming web for the topic "recycling," starting with those intriguing garbage-eating worms from my newspaper topics.

Webbing is an attractive visual metaphor, but simple brainstorming will also work, with the teacher or a scribe writing down questions as quickly as the class raises them. Small groups can work on a single topic, or after the whole class has agreed on a few key ideas, groups can develop subtopics. I also like the flexible use of index cards or small slips of paper for students to write questions on, one idea to a card. The cards can be sorted and posted on the bulletin board, patterned like a web, or grouped into related categories to provide focus for study.

If you are already well into computer use and have enough computers, kids can brainstorm for ideas using a file or hypercard program that will let them do sifting and sorting in the computer. I've also had some fun inviting students to do visual brainstorming using graphics programs to spin out their ideas in wonderfully elaborate boxes and diagrams. Computers don't necessarily improve the quality of ideas, but they may make management of them much simpler.

Categorizing

The sorting out of questions is important. In webbing, each strand or string of questions will often form a natural category. The recycling web, for example, shows four categories within the topic:

- things that eat stuff
- our community
- statistics and numbers
- commercial recycling

I ask my students to look for "big questions," questions that include other, smaller ideas and topics. Thus the question "What kinds of bugs or microscopic creatures eat waste?" can include the garbage-eating worms and open up exploration of a variety of living recyclers. An even broader question might be "Are there natural ways to recycle?" That could open up the discussion to nature's life cycles and to decay cycles that don't require animal life (for example, using ashes to create lighter, fluffier soil).

Identifying research questions

Eventually I lead students to list the major questions they want to study. There may be a single question for each student in the class, or there may be half a dozen questions which groups or the class as a whole want to investigate.

I wish I could offer you a guaranteed formula for helping students center on good "researchable" questions, but it's largely an intuitive operation. If you need to cover prescribed material, you may want to begin the list with some of the questions that are central to your objectives. However, it's important for the students to feel some commitment to their questions. I've seen groups develop apparently wonderful research questions which, in the end, nobody was interested in studying.

In calling these "research questions," I don't mean to imply that they must have formal research language phrasing — although high school juniors and seniors can certainly do some of that. Rather, what's important are good, juicy questions that fire the imagination, questions that make us say, "Yeah, I want to know more about that."

3. Finding resources

Obviously, the next step in the process is to search for answers.

Describing what we know

People seldom ask questions in a complete vacuum. You have to know a little bit about something in order to frame questions about it. Sometimes that knowledge will come from a textbook chapter, a film or television program, or a story or poem that the teacher reads aloud. But youngsters also bring their own unique knowledge to school, and we need to tap that knowledge, value it, and put it to work.

Even before doing a web, we might ask "Who knows anything about recycling?" and get that down on a transparency or a set of index cards. Of course, not all the knowledge students bring will be accurate, so teachers must be watchful and tactful in helping to sift out misinformation. Yet kids know the oddest and strangest things and make the most unexpected connections. In our recycling unit, one student had an uncle who was in the landfill business. Another had just watched his family's septic tank being rebuilt because the microbes weren't doing their job. One student collected newspapers to recycle for cash and another had heard in a vague sort of way about how buffalo droppings can be used for fuel. I used all that as part of our information base.

Intellectual scavenging

I use an activity I call an "intellectual scavenger hunt" to help students recognize the wealth of information available on almost any topic. We choose a topic for inquiry, brainstorm for questions, then brainstorm for places where answers might be found. I'm always ready with a few suggestions of my own to add. Then, in the fashion of the party game, the students disappear, notebook in hand, to see what they can learn in a short period of time, say twenty-four hours or over a weekend.

Among the resources I suggest to my students are:

Print

I'm an English teacher, so right away I point out the convenience, portability, and availability of books and magazines. Too often, I'm afraid, students have been intimidated by libraries, sent there only to do reports — looking up things in an encyclopedia and copying them. This is not the place to go on at length about library use, but I do want to say that, from kindergarten on up, we need to do a more successful job of helping kids see libraries as tools of inquiry rather than mausoleums of dusty tomes. This scavenger hunt (and interdisciplinary inquiry generally) helps students develop a different view of libraries: they become puzzles or treasure troves, places where you can tease out whatever information you need.

Non-print media

Of course, libraries contain more than just books, and many of our students are more in tune with other media. I have learned to celebrate the availability of ideas and facts in such forms as cassettes, videos, films, picture files, computer retrieval systems, and bulletin boards. Most school and public libraries have some or all of the newer storage forms, including incredible new digital systems that put visual, audio, and print material together in interactive hypertext form. The student searching for information on recycling, for example, might come back with anything from a PBS video cassette to the telephone number for a local computer network for recyclers.

Artifacts

One can also learn from objects: buildings, tools, equipment, leisure time items, things people save in their attics, things people carry to the dump (this last was especially interesting as we discussed recycling). Our scavenger hunt invariably leads to the discovery of "objects that tell a story" about the people who made them, discovered them, found them useful in their lives.

Human resources

A journalist taught me that perhaps the quickest way to find information on any topic is simply to "ask somebody who knows." Our communities are filled with specialists and experts, both amateur and professional, who can provide youngsters with answers. The Yellow Pages, as mentioned in the previous chapter, are especially helpful here. Our scavenger hunts often begin with a survey of the phone book to find, or remind ourselves of, the human resources available. Students quickly discover that they can compile massive amounts of information in short order by quizzing people in the know, either in person or by phone. And often such people are delighted to come to school to deliver a talk, show their collections, or present information.

Institutions and businesses

The Yellow Pages also remind us of places where we can go for information. Of course, institutions are primarily valuable because of the people who work and study in them. But students can learn quickly by visiting museums, local businesses, government agencies, nonprofit and public service agencies, and so on. On the topic of recycling, students can study museum exhibits, talk to businesses about their recycling efforts, discover local business people who are earning a living from recycling, learn about governmental efforts and regulations, and collect pamphlets and fliers from citizen action groups.

I want to stress that not every interdisciplinary topic needs to be exhaustively researched in this way. But even when teaching a single lesson, on the origins of World War II, for example, or on the origins of life, you can run through a mental checklist of resources and ask, "What new and different materials can I bring in on this topic?"

4. Conducting research

Just as our research questions needn't be phrased in formal, academic ways, "conducting research" need not imply scientists in white coats and face masks conducting exotic experiments.

I define research as "what you do when your initial resources give out." That is, if your questions have not been fully answered after checking the library, talking to people, and exploring Yellow Pages, it's time to roll up your sleeves and figure things out for yourself.

Kindergartners can do research as easily as senior high students. I won't detail the steps or processes of research here. I've discussed that in a book for young people (*The Young Learner's Handbook,* Scribner's, 1987), and you can scavenge up any number of good books and other materials on approaches to research (for kids) at your local library.

On our topic of recycling, for example, students can do (and have done) projects such as the following:

- interviewing community members to get their real thoughts on environmental issues and problems;
- conducting a survey to determine what percentage of community members recycle;
- inventing various ways to make recycling easier for their families;
- creating imaginative uses for recycled material and presenting those ideas to a local business person for discussion;
- putting garbage into a plastic bag, sealing it, and coming back later to see what has transpired;
- burying a recyclable plastic garbage bag to see what happens.

Such research isn't limited to any particular field or discipline. Youngsters can do it during the language arts period, as part of social studies, or for their annual science project. For the elementary teacher in a self-contained classroom, research provides a natural way to show the integration of learning. In middle schools and high schools with divided subjects, it's a way of showing that the disciplines aren't isolated from one another.

5. Synthesizing and sharing knowledge

Record keeping is an important part of any Quest learning. Once again reflecting my English teaching background, I favor having students use writing as a mode of learning. If youngsters keep notebooks, logs, journals, diaries, research notes, etc., they solidify their learning as they write, formulating and reformulating ideas. In particular, if they are working on self-selected projects and questions (rather than answering textbook study questions), their writing provides opportunity for synthesis and deepened understanding. However, students can also benefit from keeping records on cassette tapes, through photographs and videos, and in files of clippings, leaflets, and correspondence.

There comes a time when students need to pull it all together and share what they know. Too often sharing in school is done in a traditional form — "the report" — which often turns out to be encyclopedia-cribbed language copied down and inserted into a nice cover.

Copyright © 1989 by Universal Press Syndicate. Reprinted by permission.

There are, however, more energizing ways for students to put together their knowledge and present it to others. For example, students can:

- create posters and displays (the model presented by science fairs is useful here);

- give speeches, talks, and demonstrations (not typical five-minute speeches, but presentations in which they communicate what they have learned as dramatically as possible, through audio-visual aids, computer displays, etc.);
- create media projects (videos, photo displays, slide-tape presentations, computer programs and shows);
- write (newspaper articles, how-to pamphlets, informational brochures, letters to editors, letters to politicians, dramatic presentations, even fiction and poetry that express their ideas).

I find this sharing and presentation stage of the Quest model enormously exciting and satisfying. I generally use a "country fair" approach, with students setting up displays or projects or coming center stage to do demonstrations. I sit back, enjoy, learn, and observe the learning that has taken place in the students.

Other interdisciplinary teaching models

Interdisciplinary studies are so diverse that, in some respects, it's inadvisable to speak of "models" at all, particularly if they are taken to be something restricting, obligatory, or inviolable. The components that I've suggested for the Quest model are, I believe, a good representation of how learners learn anything — from initial curiosity, through information gathering, to synthesizing and sharing results. Those elements can appear in many different permutations and combinations, shaped by pupil interests, curriculum demands, school and community resources, and that inevitable category called "miscellaneous unanticipated goings on." Other writers have presented related views of the interdisciplinary process, and I want to supply overviews of two of them to supplement the Quest model.

Forrestal model

Peter Forrestal of Waneroo High School, Western Australia, has described a five-step planning process which grew from an innovative school project in Australia (in Tchudi, *English Teachers at Work*. Exeter, NH: Boynton Cook, 1986, pp. 242-245). The five stages of his model are:

Input

The teacher provides a core of information on a topic, including text chapters, field trips, library reading, films and videos, etc.

Exploration

Students — individually, in small groups, or as a whole class — take off on their own to research and discuss particular questions and issues they have raised.

Reshaping

The students work with information in some new way, moving toward synthesis and the next stage.

Presentation

New knowledge is demonstrated to the whole class.

Reflection

Teacher and students review, not only what was learned, but how the students went about learning it successfully.

The similarities and differences between this and the Quest model are apparent. The fifth stage, reflection, seems to me to be an especially valuable idea, as is the notion in the first stage that the teacher should be active in presenting students with a core of materials to get them started.

Jacobs model

In her monograph *Interdisciplinary Curriculum: Design and Implementation* (Alexandria, VA: Association for Supervision and Curriculum Development, 1990), Heidi Hayes Jacobs uses a model for teacher-prepared units which is also similar to the Quest and Australian designs. Her four stages include:

Selecting an organizing center

The teacher selects a theme, subject area, event, issue, or problem as the focus of study.

Brainstorming for associations

The teacher employs a webbing strategy to find connections between the central subject and each disciplinary area involved: mathematics, science, the arts, language arts, social studies, humanities, philosophy, etc.

Establishing guiding questions to serve as scope and sequence

Working within their own disciplines or with interdisciplinary teams, teachers design a series of questions to be answered by the study.

Writing activities for implementation

The curriculum makers develop goals, methods, and materials for helping students answer questions.

In contrast to the Quest and Australian models, Jacobs' approach is more teacher centered, more deductive. It is probably useful, in that respect, for a teacher who may be new to interdisciplinary studies and who has some reservations about turning students loose on question-asking and research prematurely.

In addition, Jacobs' second stage, where teachers systematically review the potential contributions of various disciplines, can be helpful in guaranteeing that fundamental curricular goals are covered. At the same time, it has the negative side-effect of stressing disciplinary separateness rather than my own favored goal of holistic, integrated learning. One could do stage two not only using the standard school disciplines, but also keeping in mind the alphabet of fields and disciplines on page 18.

A model for individual lessons

I have said already that you don't have to create full-blown units of several weeks or months in order to teach interdisciplinarily. It is possible to proceed quite satisfactorily and indefinitely on a smaller scale. In the heydey of the open-classroom movement, Herbert Kohl used to advise teachers to introduce freedom and choice in their classrooms a little at a time. The same is true of interdisciplinary inquiry. Instead of plunging directly into the large scale unit, you could:

- invite students to spend ten minutes thinking of questions not answered by their textbook ;
- occasionally ask students to "think outside" a discipline — for example, by figuring out a real-world application of a math problem, considering the social implications of a scientific idea, or considering the history of science;
- start a newspaper clipping file on topics in any subject or field you are teaching;
- invite students to create their own study questions or examination questions;
- bring in a guest speaker to supplement a textbook unit; or
- have the students interview a community specialist in an area of the curriculum.

The following sample provides a model for developing an individual interdisciplinary lesson, one that arises out of a concept within a single discipline. If you have a specific idea to teach in social studies or geography or math, for example, this sample suggests a rubric that encourages learners to think outside the limits of the discipline and reach for other connections. Although few experienced teachers write formal lesson plans that spell out objectives, materials, procedures, etc., new teachers may find it helpful to construct a few lessons following this model as a way of becoming improvisational and naturally interdisciplinary in any lesson.

An interdisciplinary lesson model

Goals

1. List goals, aims, or objectives for the specific component of disciplinary knowledge you wish to teach (e.g., the three principle forms of the lever).

2. Brainstorm for secondary goals reflecting an interdisciplinary perspective, using Jacobs' stage two technique. List two or three interrelated goals (e.g., how levers function in construction, "leverage" as a political/social metaphor).

Materials

In addition to the text, list possible or known resources from the library, the audio-visual collection, community members, institutions, artifacts. Plan to use at least one non-text source in the lesson.

Procedures

Develop a split-column list of your teaching procedures, key questions, student input, etc. Place those connected with the central (disciplinary) goal in the left column, possible interdisciplinary connections on the right. In this way you force yourself to remain conscious of the interdisciplinary aspects of your teaching.

Teaching the concept	Interdisciplinary aspects
The lever: How does it work?	Let's move that big stone off the playground!

Evaluation

Evaluate the core or disciplinary concept by your usual means: summary of the lesson, student recap, quality of discussion, answers to study questions. Then have students consider interdisciplinary questions.

Interdisciplinary extensions

What does this idea have to do with the rest of the world? What applications can you see in real life? How might this concept be useful in other classes or units you are studying? What questions does this provoke? Where, outside of this discipline, can you find more answers?

Questions and answers

Here are some questions I am often asked by teachers who are getting started with interdisciplinary teaching. My answers have grown from my own experiences — both successes and misadventures — and are intended to be work-in-progress, not complete or definitive responses. As you explore interdisciplinary studies, you'll come up with answers of your own, often more complex than mine, and certainly better suited to your own teaching situation.

Question: What about coverage of the required curriculum? It would be nice to spend two months on a topic like winter or the four elements, but I have a text (or a curriculum guide) to cover, which specifies what is to be learned.

Answer: I think it's very important to recall that in the field of education, "coverage" has never worked all that well in the first place. We cover, but do they learn? Still, I fully recognize that there is often a curriculum and that one is expected to do it justice. I think it's useful to begin interdisciplinary teaching by examining the course or curriculum guide, ferreting out goals and objectives. Then you can look for interdisciplinary topics or themes that encompass them. Interdisciplinary philosophy does not argue that segmented knowledge is necessarily "bad" or "wrong," just that it's most often presented in too narrow a context. We might call the interdisciplinary program, then, "curriculum plus." You cover not only the basics, but the basics and a lot more.

If you're teaching quadratic equations, for instance, find some topics or problems in society that actually use quadratics for solution and build from that. If you're studying a historical period or era, look for connections between that era and what has happened in your own community. Remember how Sybil Marshall turned that deadly dull Rome unit into local English history. Did her kids understand Rome? My bet is that she "covered" what they needed to know.

Question: There's also the question of time: the curriculum is already filled to the brim. How do I find the time to do the in-depth work that the interdisciplinary method seems to require?

Answer: My answer is another question: time for what? For generations educators have debated intensive vs. extensive education, depth vs. coverage. Other teachers debated process vs. content, or global skills vs. explicit knowledge. I don't think we have to make either/or decisions here, and I believe that interdisciplinary inquiry gives us a way out of the dilemma.

Yes, teaching from an interdisciplinary perspective does require more classroom time. However, my claim (and you can check me on this one in your own classroom) is that the additional time gives high yield benefits in depth, coverage, process, and knowledge. A well-constructed unit or lesson covers far more than the minimums, and it often gets students deeply engaged in the processes of learning, so they know how to learn on their own. (I can hear a question on evaluation and assessment being formulated, but I'll come back to that topic later.)

Further, one often finds that topics which were formerly isolated in textbook chapters begin to flow together. In the last answer, for example, I proposed taking quadratic equations "to the street." The math teachers I know who've done that find that community-based learning covers a big chunk of the curriculum all at once. You can't limit life to quadratics; pretty soon decimals worm their way in, fractions show up on your teaching doorstep, graphs demand to be done. Just as an interdisciplinary unit requires more time than a textbook chapter, it also covers far more than that chapter.

Question: I'm not a renaissance person. I don't know everything there is to know about math, science, language arts, social studies, and myriad other topics in the encyclopedia. How do you expect me to teach in all these fields?

Answer: First, my own experience tells me that teachers know a lot more about many fields than they sometimes think. Most of us entered teaching because we were curious people and good learners to begin with, so don't sell your background short.

More important, inquiry learning helps us see that it's not necessary for the teacher always to play "answerman" or "answerwoman," to be Ms. or Mr. Wizard. When you recognize that your own background is a bit shaky, look for help from the outside — or inside. Your primary skill is helping kids learn to learn, not simply feeding them answers. You can help students locate books, find resources, think of problems and questions, organize their answers. Let them do the work of learning.

I admit that it takes a bit of courage the first few times you approach teaching this way. Once I got over my initial nervousness at not being a universal, omniscient, ubiquitous information machine, I came to delight in helping students with projects where I don't have much background. I've learned a great deal in the process, both directly from my students and indirectly from helping them figure out how to learn a new field.

I also advocate taking on the role of teacher/learner. Acknowledge to students that you don't know everything, pick an aspect of the topic that interests you, and, either alone or with some students, do some learning yourself. I've come to relish this role, and playing it from time to time helps me remain in tune with the kinds of problems my students are experiencing.

Question: My school is low on resources. The library is poor; we don't have many computers; we don't have much in the way of audio-visual equipment, much less AV materials. What do I do?

Answer: Try a variation of the intellectual scavenger hunt, focusing on what's available in your community that's free or inexpensive. Even schools and public libraries with apparently limited resources often have untapped riches: top shelves in closets full of treasures, reference texts you've never heard of, files of clippings, a drawerful of cassette tapes, exchange agreements with other libraries in your region, access to the state/provincial libraries. Ask your own school librarian, who will likely be eager to have somebody use more stuff.

Are you short of AV materials? Look to your local video outlets, which probably outnumber libraries ten to one. Risk a couple of dollars of your own funds to enrich your class with an appropriate classic film or documentary. Or develop the habit of scanning the television guide a week in advance for shows relevant to your study — you'll be amazed how many connections you can make — and assign your students some television to watch.

I've already praised the newspaper. Bring yours into the class daily, and at a cost of pennies, you'll find abundant materials to use. Also, talk to the parent-teacher group about funding small classroom libraries on interdisciplinary topics. Ask your local magazine distributor about getting some freebies. Above all, turn the kids loose and watch what they come up with, even in the smallest of backwater towns.

Question: Several of the projects you've described talk about getting out into the town or taking field trips. Here again our resources are very limited. I can't take kids to museums or science centers.

Answer: As desirable as those trips are, they're not absolutely vital to the program. Television, used well, is a surrogate form of the field trip. So is a trip to the library, or a telephone call. (By the way, check the library for a directory of toll free numbers, which will allow students — in North America, at least — to get all sorts of free information from businesses and industries.) Also look into the use of computer bulletin boards and electronic information services. Ours has become an electronic global village, so let the silicon chips do the walking.

Question: Scheduling team-taught classes is a nightmare in my school district. I'd really like to work with teachers in other disciplines, but I can't see how it could be worked out.

Answer: It's too bad school districts are not more committed to using their computers for such matters. The fact is that with contemporary computer technology, it's quite easy to work out very sophisticated schedules.

For the present, though, you may have to do with cruder strategies. The simplest of these is an idea that first came up in the 1930s: correlation. It simply means that teachers agree to correlate or orchestrate their study. This can take place across disciplines (a high school science and an English class) or even classrooms (two second grade classes, possibly in different school buildings). You work interdisciplinarily and exchange information and results from time to time. Or you exchange teachers rather than students. Scheduling classes back-to-back, which gives teachers a sustained period of time to work, is sometimes possible.

But it's important to emphasize, too, that interdisciplinary teaching does not require team-taught classes. In fact, in many respects it's better done by a single teacher rather than (once again) having instruction fragmented by specialties.

Question: You've made bold claims for interdisciplinary teaching. Does it really engage all kids in productive independent learning?

Answer: No. And I certainly don't want to be guilty of promoting it as some sort of magical cure. There are some kids who don't work very well in this kind of classroom, for a variety of reasons. Occasionally I've run across bright students who hate it. Ironically, they've gotten so good at following instructions, mastering textbooks, and taking tests that they don't want anything other than routine. And there are kids who have been so burned out by schooling, or who are so unmotivated, that nothing — not even building a nuclear device — would rouse them.

My philosophy is to give such students all the attention they have a right to, and to keep chipping away at their interests. I've never met a student yet who wasn't interested in something outside of school which could be connected, by hook or by crook, to an interdisciplinary unit. Let me concede again that, no, I haven't always been able to reach every last student. In general, however, I find attention and interest levels far higher in interdisciplinary classes than in others.

Question: This kind of work is highly individualized. How does one keep from going nuts with thirty-five or so kids doing their own thing?

Answer: Most of us were probably nuts to become teachers in the first place. Of course it can get pretty complex. I find visual organizers like webs a helpful way of keeping track of the big pattern. I make charts that can be posted on the wall for everyone to see. A miniaturized version goes into my gradebook or teaching notes. In my classes we usually start with one common topic, web our way to create small groups, then have people individualize. Finally we come together again for a whole class show'n'tell. This nesting approach makes a project more manageable than truly having every kid on a unique endeavor.

I also emphasize that students — even the youngest — need to keep records. Help students learn to be accountable, just as you're helping them learn how to learn. I recommend a folder for each student, into which go notes, lists, titles of books read, progress reports on projects, etc.

I find such records also useful in documenting what we've done — which gets back to the coverage question mentioned earlier. Bongo teachers keep lists of the key concepts that each unit covers in such areas as English, math, science, history, health and physical education, and so on. A carefully kept list is often quite dazzling. An interdisciplinary teacher can often not only claim to have covered the required components in a particular discipline, but a good chunk of the curriculum for other disciplines as well.

Question: The approach also seems to call for students who are independent self-starters. Isn't that a bit naive, given today's youngsters?

Answer: I think the difficulty lies more in patterns of schooling than in the nature of children. The youngest students in our pre-schools and schools show remarkable curiosity and motivation. By the time they hit senior high school, they seem bored and reluctant to try new things. Some of that is due to shifting interests and a natural desire to be out in the world, but much of it comes from teaching — discipline-centered teaching — which drives out independence of mind.

I'm more worried about the naivete of a teacher who would plunge into an elaborate student-centered unit and assume that the youngsters already have the necessary skills. In reality, a good bit of the "teaching" in interdisciplinary inquiry is required, as indicated in the title of a book by Crawford Lindsey: *Teaching Students to Teach Themselves* (London and New York: Kogan Page/Nichols, 1988). This book discusses ways of guiding students into successfully pursuing their own projects; I found it very helpful. Another helpful title is Garth Boomer's *Negotiating the Curriculum: A Teacher Student Partnership* (Sydney: Ashton Scholastic, 1984).

Question: What about grading?

Answer: I struggle with grading in all my classes, not just interdisciplinary ones. In my ideal world, we'd get rid of letter grades and substitute a pass/fail or credit/no credit system. I am envious of the freedom of many elementary school teachers to teach without the anxiety of trying to reduce all assessment to a monolithic symbol. In secondary school and college, I prefer contract grading, where the more students do, the higher their grade. Contracts favor the busy beavers who can crank out work at a great rate. But contracts are also good for less dazzling learners: a contract makes it clear exactly what you have to do to earn a grade.

In an interdisciplinary class, I generally have minimum requirements for a grade of C (or its equivalent), and one or two additional levels of work required to earn a B or an A. Usually the extra contract work centers on individual reading, research, or other activities related to our core theme. For guidance with a contract system, I recommend *Using Contract Grading* (Malcolm Knowles, San Francisco: Jossey Bass, 1986).

I also find that the sort of documentation discussed in a previous question genuinely helps make grading easier for the teacher. If students' work has been well and thoroughly documented throughout an interdisciplinary unit, determining and defending grades is simpler.

Other questions? Comments? I'd be pleased to correspond with teachers who have worked with ideas growing from this book. Write to me c/o Department of English, University of Nevada, Reno, NV 89557, USA.

A potpourri of interdisciplinary teaching ideas

What follows is a collection of ideas briefly presented — hints and suggestions for possible use in interdisciplinary teaching. They are not arranged in any particular order, and I leave it to you to fit them into your own teaching if and as you wish. For each starter idea I invite you to see how many different disciplines you feel could be brought to bear on a project and/or to see how specific concepts from particular disciplines could be taught through it.

For example, the first idea has students research the science behind everyday phenomena. While such a project might begin in the science class, it can easily be connected with such subjects as mathematics (charts, statistics, creating formulae), language arts (note-taking, creating a booklet or display), history (the origins of various common devices and machines), social science (the impact of various scientific inventions on how we live), health and physical education (the science of exercise and diet), and geography (the "home countries" of various scientific discoveries). In the end, "science in everyday life" could be taught in almost any classroom, from kindergarten to grade twelve, under a variety of interdisciplinary configurations.

Science in everyday life

In his book *Science in Everyday Life* (New York: Harper & Row, 1980), William Vergara offers explanations of the scientific principles behind everyday actions: boiling water, tying your shoes, eating breakfast. Have students investigate their own questions about familiar phenomena and gizmos. (Vergara also has a companion volume doing the same thing with mathematics.)

Needed inventions

What do we need around the house, around the school, in the world? Investigate and report on these ideas, perhaps including demonstrations of simulated or working models.

Folklore and superstition

Investigate and reflect upon some of the folk traditions in students' lives, and discuss the science and culture behind them.

Magic and illusion

Study the history of magic and the nature of illusion, including the math, science, psychology, and linguistics that make them successful. Create a magic show or a classroom parlor of illusions.

Collections

A good collection — stamps, soft drink or beer cans, butterflies — is a museum in itself, if ordered, labeled, and presented so that other people can learn from it.

Measurement

Throw out the existing standard measures of height, weight, distance, time. Invent new ones to quantify your school or your town.

Letters

Probe the interdisciplinary world with letters to editors, politicians, folk heroes/heroines, Nobel Prize winners, poets laureate, authors, relatives, pen pals in other lands . . .

Games

Designing a game calls for a great range of thinking skills, background knowledge, and practical understanding of human nature. Try designing games that cover themes or topics in science, geography, social studies, language arts, physical education, art . . .

Cross-age teaching

Consider the interdisciplinary skills required for, say, a fourth grader to teach an idea to a first grader. Or cut across age lines on any disciplinary project. Imagine senior citizens and kindergartners looking into recycling or animal intelligence.

Computer programing

Computer whizzes in any class can help a teacher design games, activities, quizzes, simulations, bibliographies and resource lists.

Science fiction

Knowledge can be usefully shared by imagining what will happen in the future. Consider the possibilities for recycling or animal intelligence in the year 3001, for example.

Community problems

Identify some of the major problems and/or issues your community faces. Organize, brainstorm, work in teams, and come up with solutions.

Space

What is humankind's future in space? What does the exploration of space help us learn? What do you have to know from interdisciplinary perspectives in order to explore and understand space?

Preservation

Find something old in your town and learn where it came from, why it's important, what you can do to preserve it.

Questions

Create a question box in the classroom and open it from time to time. The questions you can't answer can form the focus for interdisciplinary research.

Medicine

What is sickness? Where does it come from? What are the major illnesses we face in our lifetime? What's the history of medicine?

The Greeks

Who were these folks, and why do textbooks have so much to say about them?

Evolution and scientism

What are the central issues under discussion in these two systems? Can we find people to argue both sides for us?

Chocolate chip cookie mining

Give students a chocolate chip cookie and ten minutes to remove as many chips as they can without destroying the "environment" of the cookie. Use this as a jumping off point for an ecology unit. (I picked up this idea at a National Science-Technology-Society conference, but I've lost the reference. My apologies to the originator.)

Bag it

Bring in a diverse collection of bags — shopping bags, junk food bags, plastic bags, large sacks, tiny envelopes. Have students create a museum display which explains the relationships and classifications of bags. (Thanks to Katarina Cerny, Henry Ford Museum, Dearborn, Michigan.)

Soda poppery

My book of the same title (New York: Charles Scribner's Sons, 1986) grew from an interdisciplinary study based on my curiosity about soft drinks and how to make them at home.

Messing about in science

David Hawkings encourages us to let students design some of their own experiments (within reasonable limits), to make mistakes, to change procedures, to find solutions to their own questions — this in preference to "canned" laboratory projects (*Science and Children*, February 1965, 58-70).

Perpetual motion

Invent machines for same. (Don't forget to turn your machine off when you're finished!)

Clay

Have some available at all times to make models of machines, biological structures, inventions, faces of characters in literature, historical buildings, etc.

Glass

Study its composition, effects, uses, and imagery, its connections with science, mathematics, social studies, and literature.

What if . . .?

Integrate science, history, and math by asking this question: What if Thomas Edison had not developed the light bulb in the late nineteenth century? What if nuclear fission had not been discovered? What if the land bridge between Asia and North America had not sunk into the sea? (Thanks to Mary Lynn Nama for this idea.)

Role play

Dramatize great moments in science, in math. Do "you are there" scenes of historical moments. Bring historical figures to life in the classroom.

Blockbusters

Give older students a list of the breakthrough thinkers in a field or discipline: Newton, Darwin, Curie, Galileo. Have them research these thinkers' ideas and place them in historical, cultural, and literary contexts.

Create an assembly line

Give students blocks and the assignment to create various parts of a larger structure. Assign a corporate leader, line worker, foreman, and engineer. Allow a limited period of time for students to complete structures or to compete for contracts. Use this as a jumping off point for an interdisciplinary unit on labour, technology, society. (Thank you, Steve Hicks.)

Sports statistics

Let students keep elaborate statistics on their favorite sports. (Thank you more, Steve Hicks.)

The dig

Engage students in historical or social studies work by finding and examining primary documents only: diaries, journals, newspaper accounts, interviews. Help them discover how history is created.

Debate

Set up mini-debates (with very short speeches and rebuttals), formal debates, or written debates on topics in virtually any disciplinary/ interdisciplinary issue.

Poem as science

A poem, like a piece of scientific research, tries to describe things "as they really are." Explore that metaphor.

Graduation day

Have older students design a set of thoughtful questions which they would like to be asked (or to ask one another) on the day they graduate from high school.

Time capsule

Select artifacts and create a time capsule for kids in your school to open twenty-five years in the future. Have students include written reports, drawings, and photographs which explain the artifacts and the reasons for including them in the capsule.

The eye of the camera

Study a collection of photographs to see how a photographer can "make a statement" with his/her camera. Then research a topic such as flowers, the school, people, or places. Use cameras as the tool for recording information. Whether students use still photos, video, or film, have them determine what sorts of generalizations they can make from visual images. They can also compare how different photographic media differ in their potential to record detail. A good interdisciplinary spinoff project is to interest students in the technology of film and images, including some darkroom work.

The eye of the painter

Do the same sort of activity based on great (or not so great) works of art. What does a painter tell us about the society/world in which he or she lives? Also, as Sybil Marshall did, have students learn to use visual symbols in addition to written words to record ideas.

The story of writing

Do the same sort of activity based on great (or not so great) writings. What does a writer tell us about the world? How does your own writing allow you to understand and record the world you see about you? As a spinoff, study the origins of writing, from pictographs to (western) alphabets or (eastern) characters.

Engines

Take several apart. Reconstruct them. Learn the history of their energy sources. Predict their future.

The day you were born

Have students research the history, science, technology, and reading of the year when they were born.

Organizations and publications

This is by no means an exhaustive list. It is simply a sample of the kinds of groups that share an interest in integrated education. Many of them publish newsletters or journals. Write to them for current subscription information.

Association for Canadian Studies (P.O. Box 8888, Station A, Montreal, Quebec, H3C 3P8) A multi-disciplinary association that publishes the ASC Newsletter, which focuses especially on the social sciences and humanities.

Association for Media Literacy (40 McArthur Street, Weston, Ontario, M9P 3M7) Develops resources in media literacy. Workshops, a newsletter and an anthology are available for teachers.

Agency for Tele-Education (P.O. Box 200, Station Q, Toronto, Ontario M4T 2T1) Umbrella group for educational TV across Canada. Has an annual publication available in both English and French.

Agora (P.O. Box 10975, Raleigh, North Carolina 27605-0975) An outstanding interdisciplinary magazine designed for high ability junior and senior high school students. Combines literature, science, and the arts in exploring issues from a thematic perspective.

Assembly on Science and Humanities (National Council of Teachers of English, 1111 Kenyon Road, Urbana, Illinois 61801) A group emphasizing integrated, interdisciplinary study through the medium of language. Publishes a quarterly newsletter.

Association for Experiential Education (University of Colorado, Box 249, Boulder, Colorado 80309) A network of people worldwide interested in "hands in" learning. Membership includes a journal, newsletters, and a membership directory.

Bongo (Middle College High School, 31-10 Thomson Avenue, Long Island City, New York 11101) See description on pages 29-30.

Canadian Association for Co-operative Education (Suite 203, 1209 King Street West, Toronto, Ontario, M6K 1G2) Focuses on post-secondary co-operative education. Produces both directories and handbooks.

Canadian Association for Curriculum Studies (c/o Faculty of Education, Queen's University, Kingston, Ontario K7G 3N6) An organization for educators interested in curriculum research, with a special interest in language arts, social education and science. Newsletter; also conference procedings titled "Curriculum Canada."

Canadian Book Information Centre (260 King Street East, Toronto, Ontario, M5A 1K3) Produces a newsletter that provides all types of book and book-related information.

Canadian Council for Multicultural and Intercultural Education (Suite 204, 316 Dalhousie Street, Ottawa, Ontario K1N 7B7) Serves both public and private sectors. Produces a journal three times annually.

Cooperative Learning Center (202 Pattee Hall, University of Minnesota, Minneapolis, Minnesota 55455) Publishes "The Cooperative Link," a newsletter providing a network for teachers interested in small group learning.

Global Education Associates (Suite 456, 475 Riverside Drive, New York, New York 10115) Publishes "Breakthrough," a quarterly newsletter linking educators concerned with global education and intercultural understanding.

Holistic Education Review (P.O. Box 1476, Greenfield, Massachusetts 01302) A superb professional journal with an emphasis on "human fulfillment, global cooperation, and ecological responsibility" through integrated studies.

Institute for Democracy in Education (119 McCracken Hall, College of Education, Ohio University, Athens, Ohio 45701-2979) Focuses on ways of empowering students as learners. Publishes a quarterly journal and a membership bulletin.

Institute for Learning and Teaching (449 Desnoyer, St. Paul, Minnesota 55104) Publishes "The Brain-Based Educational Networker," a newsletter focusing on whole-brain learning and the implications for schooling.

National Association for Core Curriculum (404 White Hall, Kent State University, Kent, Ohio 44242) Dedicated to interdisciplinary instruction with a focus on the humanities. Publishes a newsletter, "The Core Teacher."

National Association for Science, Technology, and Society (117 Willard Building, University Park, Pennsylvania 16802) Publishes a journal and newsletter, and holds an outstanding national conference for teachers interested in bridging the two-culture gap.

National Film Board of Canada (P.O. Box 6100, Station A, Montreal, Quebec, H3C 3H5) Provides films and videos for interdisciplinary studies. Issues regular reports.

Ontario Institute for Studies in Education (252 Bloor Street West, Toronto, Ontario M5S 1V5) Conducts a variety of interdisciplinary projects, and publishes some teaching units.

Renaissance Educational Associates (4817 N. County Road 29, Loveland, Colorado 80538) Focuses on the renaissance ideals of integrated education. Publishes a quarterly newsletter and offers a variety of AV aids and summer workshops.

Youth Science Foundation (Room 904, 151 Slater Street, Ottawa, Ontario, K1P 5H3) Promotes science literacy and encourages young people to consider careers in science and technology. Publishes a report six times a year.

The *Bright Idea* Series

In *Bright Idea* books, gifted authors reveal to readers the hearts of their professional lives. What has excited them professionally? What have they spent their years discovering, and why?

In these books they dress some old truths in new styles, and reveal some new truths about children, about language, about learning, about teachers, teaching and parenting.

The series was conceived and is published in Canada, but the authors come from all over: the United States, New Zealand, The Netherlands, Great Britain, Canada.

In Canada, order from Scholastic Canada Ltd., 123 Newkirk Road, Richmond Hill, Ontario L4C 3G5.

In the United States, order from Scholastic Inc., P.O. Box 7502, Jefferson City, MO 65102.

☞   Available in New Zealand and Australia through Ashton Scholastic, and in the United Kingdom through Scholastic Publications.